The Pastor's Guide
To
Wise Investing

S.L. POTTS

2018 Edition

Requests for information should be addressed to:
admin@brokepastor.com.

This publication is designed to provide competent and reliable information regarding the subject matter covered. However, it is sold with the understanding that the author and publisher are not engaged in rendering legal, accounting, financial, or other professional advice. Laws and practices often vary state to state and country to country, and if legal or other expert assistance is required, the services of a competent professional person should be sought. The author and publisher specifically disclaim any liability that is incurred from the use or application of the contents of this book. From a Declaration of Principles jointly adopted by a Committee of the American Bar Association and a Committee of Publishers and Associations.

Original and modified cover art by Stacy Potts and CoverDesignStudio.com.

Unless otherwise noted, Scripture quotations are from the ESV® Bible (The Holy Bible, English Standard Version®), copyright © 2001 by Crossway, a publishing ministry of Good News Publishers. Used by permission. All rights reserved.

ISBN-13: 978-0-9994737-0-2

Visit our website, www.brokepastor.com.

To Nathaniel and Hannah. May you always listen to those older and wiser than you. I love you both.

Table of Contents

PREFACE

I am not a certified financial advisor. I am just a pastor who has spent ten years reading and listening to people who are much smarter and more accomplished than I am when it comes to investing – people like: Warren Buffett, Jack Bogle, Benjamin Graham, etc.

Despite the amazing intellect and ability of these financial geniuses, it's amazing to me how simple and cohesive their advice about investing really is. In fact, it's so simple . . . so basic . . . that anyone can understand it and do it - even a pastor like me!

It has been my observation over the years that pastors are often very good at so many difficult things – preaching, caring, counseling – but are often not very good at handling their money wisely.

To that end, I have written this book to provide a succinct, easy-to-read compilation of some of the best investing advice from some of the best investors ever. I encourage you to read their advice carefully and to follow it diligently.

S.L. Potts
Virginia Beach, VA
August 8, 2017

CHAPTER 1
YOUR BIGGEST ENEMY

Almost everyone knows the name of Warren Buffett – maybe the greatest, most successful investor of our day. But very few people outside the world of professional investing know the name of his teacher, mentor, and friend – Benjamin Graham.

In 1950, when Buffett was just nineteen years old, he read Graham's monumental work, *The Intelligent Investor*. Buffett said that, at the time, he thought it was the best book about investing ever written.[1] Today, at eighty-six, he still believes the same thing.

Buffett writes:

> To invest successfully over a lifetime does not require a stratospheric IQ, unusual business insights, or inside information. What's needed is a sound intellectual framework for making decisions and the ability to keep emotions from corroding that framework. This book [*The Intelligent Investor*] precisely and clearly prescribes the proper framework. You must supply the emotional discipline.[2]

---

[1] Buffett, Warren E. "Preface to the Fourth Edition." In Benjamin Graham, *The Intelligent Investor – Revised Edition; Updated with New Commentary by Jason Zweig* (New York, NY: Harper Collins Publishers, 2003), ix.

[2] Ibid.

Did you notice the two components Buffett says are needed to be a successful investor? He said that you need a "sound intellectual framework" and "the ability to keep emotions from corroding that framework."

In fact, he went further and said that you do not need "a stratospheric IQ, unusual business insights, or inside information." You just need a "sound intellectual framework" and "the ability to keep emotions from corroding that framework."

This is striking to me.

As I listen to most people talk about investing, it seems that there is a common belief that the biggest enemy facing most investors is some lack of one of the three things Buffett says we do not need. Yet, almost no one ever talks about the two things he says we do need. Is it just me, or does this seem backwards?

I hope that, through the rest of this book, I will provide you with a bit of the "sound intellectual framework" that men like Graham and Buffett epitomize, but what we need to focus our attention on first is the issue of emotions and how to keep them from "corroding that framework."

A GUIDING PRINCIPLE

Why is Buffett so concerned with the potentially dangerous role emotions can play in the decision-making process of the investor? Well, to answer that question briefly, he is concerned about it because his mentor, Benjamin Graham, taught him to be concerned about it.

Listen to Graham:

> We shall say quite a bit about the psychology of investors. For indeed, the investor's chief problem – and even his worst enemy – is likely to be himself. ("The fault, dear investor, is not in our stars – and not in our stocks – but in ourselves")[3]

He goes on to say:

> By arguments, examples, and exhortation, we hope to aid our readers to establish the proper mental and emotional attitudes toward their investment decisions. We have seen much more money made and *kept* by "ordinary people" who were temperamentally well suited for the investment process than by those who lacked this quality, even though they had an extensive knowledge of finance, accounting, and stock market lore.[4]

I don't know about you, but I think that this is quite an amazing observation. "The investor's chief problem – and even his worst enemy – is likely to be himself." Let those words sink deeply into your heart and mind because I think they have the potential to change the way we think about investing entirely.

How are we our worst enemies when it comes to investing? Let me count the ways!

---

[3] Benjamin Graham, The Intelligent Investor – Revised Edition; Updated with New Commentary by Jason Zweig, 2003 (New York, NY: Harper Collins Publishers, 2003), 8.

[4] Ibid. Emphasis his.

THE DANGER OF FEAR

Without any exaggeration, fear has to be one of the greatest dangers the investor faces. Fear causes people to not invest at all, or to not invest logically, or to stop investing when they shouldn't.

First, we all want certainty and stability – two words that are never used to describe the process of investing. This causes some people to never even begin investing in the first place. They would rather avoid the uncertainty and risk of loss, despite the amazing possibilities of gain, in order to maintain some sense of stability and control.

My father had a saying about this: "Opportunity's cost is opportunity lost." If you want to take advantage of the opportunity to play it safe by staying away from investing, then the cost will be you losing the opportunity of likely making a substantial amount of money by engaging in a moderate-but-wise amount of risk through investing. You can't have both. It will be one or the other.

Second, fear causes some people to not invest logically. I prefer to think about stocks like I think about toilet paper. I'm always going to need it, and therefore, I should always buy some . . . but when should I buy a lot? When the price is high? Or when the price is low?

I can't speak for you, but I like to stock up (no pun intended) on toilet paper when it's on sale, and then only buy what I need when it's not. That seems to be a logical approach.

Yet, how do many people react when it comes to the stock market? When stocks are going up in price, they tend to buy more because they get excited and feel safer (for some unknown reason), and when stocks are going down in price, they tend to buy less (or even sell what they have) out of fear that they will continue to drop in price.

Have you ever heard the old adage: "Buy low; sell high"? While I, generally, don't agree with the selling part, I definitely agree with the buying part. When stock prices are dropping, that's the time to buy - not sit back in fear! Think of it as a sale on stocks. That's using logic.

Finally, and going along with the previous point, fear often causes people to stop investing and, worse, sell when they shouldn't.

I remember having dinner with a dear family once who started talking about their retirement. Though both were near retirement age, they said they had next to nothing saved for the future. According to them, they had gotten scared in 2008 (during the huge stock market crash), had sold all of their stock, and had never re-entered the market – even almost ten years later.

Let's think about this for a moment. Let's pretend that, at the end of 2007, they had a total retirement account of $100,000 invested in an S&P 500 index fund. If they sold after the crash of 2008, they would have only received about $63,000 – a $37,000 loss. And since they never re-entered the stock market, that $63,000 would have remained mostly unchanged to the present time.

However, had they not sold their stocks and simply stayed in the market, ignoring their fear, that same $100,000 would be worth approximately $185,000 today . . . even with the huge loss of 2008! In other words, they lost $122,000 because of nothing but fear.

Unfortunately, they are not alone. Many people listen to the "experts" who, like Chicken Little, tell them that the sky is falling and that they should "sell, sell, sell" just because the market is going down, down, down. Don't listen to the fear mongers. If you can control your emotions, you will almost certainly out-perform all those who make rash decisions due to fear.

Fear is a real danger to the investor.

THE DANGER OF PRIDE

It's amazing to me how so many people with no real knowledge about the stock market can genuinely believe that they know so much about the stock market.

I can't begin to tell you the number of people I have talked to . . . that I simply cannot talk to. They won't listen. Before the conversation even begins, it's over. They're too stubborn to listen to anyone else.

Now, a part of me gets this – particularly when it's me who's talking to them. The fact of the matter is that I don't know anything about stocks either. I'm a pastor. I went to seminary. I work for a church.

But you would think they would want to listen to Warren Buffett or Peter Lynch or Jack Bogle or any of the other truly successful investors out there who have said, over and over again with amazing unity, what it takes to be a sound investor.

If I've learned anything over a decade of pastoring people, it's that you can't help someone who doesn't want to be helped. Until a person is humble enough to admit their need and ask for help, you're wasting your time and breath on them. The same applies to investing.

I know that I don't know anything about investing, and that's the point. Because I don't know anything about investing, I've turned to those who do. I've read and studied and compiled information and advice over the years from some of the best, most successful investors of our time. Even in this book, as I said in the preface, I'm not giving you my own thoughts or advice. I'm simply providing you with the advice of others for your consideration. While you would be unwise to listen to me, you would be very wise to listen to those who have invested successfully.

Pride can be a real danger to the investor.

THE DANGER OF GREED
How much is truly enough? The answer for most people is almost always "more!" Even for pastors, the temptation to pursue wealth and money out of pure greed is real and palpable.

In 1 Timothy 6, Paul writes:

> 6 But godliness with contentment is great gain, 7 for we brought nothing into the world, and we cannot take anything out of the world. 8 But if we have food and clothing, with these we will be content. 9 But those who desire to be rich fall into temptation, into a snare, into many senseless and harmful desires that plunge people into ruin and destruction. 10 For the love of money is a root of all kinds of evils. It is through this craving that some have wandered away from the faith and pierced themselves with many pangs.

In greed, people often make foolish decisions about investing. In a desire for more and more, they begin to take unreasonable and unjustified risks. Greed drives both rich and poor to destruction.

I hope that this is not true for you. I have not written this book to help you get rich through investing, but to help you be wise. Whether God grants you plenty or want, you must learn to be content.

Greed is a real danger to the investor.

THE PATH FORWARD

Over the next few chapters, I will attempt to show you the "sound intellectual framework" that men like Buffett, Graham, and so many others have spoken of.

I sincerely believe that, if you follow it, you will be making wise decisions with your investments. But as we begin, make sure you understand that the biggest danger you face is not the uncertainty of the markets or your lack of experience/knowledge.

The biggest danger you face in the process of investing is yourself.

CHAPTER 2
A RIGHT VIEW OF STOCKS

I have never bought a stock.

If that statement seems odd given the fact that I am writing to you about how to be a wise investor, perhaps the problem lies in my terminology and not in my actions.

I never buy stocks. I always buy businesses. There is a subtle, but powerful difference in those two ideas.

In our day and age, stocks are something that can be traded in seconds . . . or less. Stocks are like commodities or services or baseball cards. You can buy them or sell them at will.

Businesses aren't like that. If you were to start a business today, you would not expect to be able to sell it tomorrow or in an hour or in a second. Businesses seem more stable and long-term in our minds than stocks do.

Well, can I blow your mind by reminding you that stocks are nothing more than individual pieces of a business? When you buy a stock, you are actually buying a business. You are becoming a business owner.

This is how you should think of yourself and of your investments. You are a business owner, and you own a collection of businesses. Seeing yourself and your investments this way will begin to play itself out in the areas listed below.

CHAPTER 3
DON'T TRY TO BEAT THE MARKET

Nobody knows what is going to happen in the stock market tomorrow or next week or next month or next quarter or next year. NO ONE.

Alexander Green has compiled a "who's who" list of experts to testify to this truth:

> Benjamin Graham, the father of value investing: "If I have noticed anything over these 60 years on Wall Street, it is that people do not succeed in forecasting what's going to happen to the stock market."

> Warren Buffett: "We've long felt that the only value of stock forecasters is to make fortune tellers look good. Even now, Charlie [Munger] and I continue to believe that short-term market forecasts are poison and should be kept locked up in a safe place, away from children and also from grown-ups who behave in the market like children."

> John Templeton, pioneer of global investing and legendary manager of the Templeton Growth Fund: "I never ask if the market is going to go up or down next year. I know there is no one who can tell me that."

> Peter Lynch, the best performing mutual fund manager of all time, in his book *One Up on Wall Street*: "Thousands of experts study overbought indicators, oversold indicators, head-and-

shoulder patterns, put-call ratios, the Fed's policy on money supply, foreign investments, the movement of the constellations through the heavens, and the moss on oak trees, and they can't predict the markets with any useful consistency any more than the gizzard squeezers could tell the Roman emperors when the Huns would attack."[5]

Now, let's think about this. If some of the best investors who have ever lived are saying, with one voice, that no one knows what the market is going to do next, do you really think some random broker, financial planner, or talking head on TV has figured out what these giants of investing haven't?

More practically (and close to home), do you really think that you or your uncle or some random guy your friend knows has been able to decode what the most brilliant minds in investing have not?

Give me a break!

This is why John Bogle, legendary founder of Vanguard®, calls trying to beat the market a loser's game.[6] For the average investor, there are simply too many variables at play for them to do it.

A better approach, Bogle would say, is to be content to track with the market through the purchase of passively-managed, index-based, mutual funds. Let's break that statement down a bit.

---

[5] Alexander Green, *The Gone Fishin' Portfolio* (Hoboken, NJ: John Wiley & Sons, Inc., 2008), 31-32.
[6] John Bogle, *The Little Book of Common Sense Investing* (Hoboken, NJ: John Wiley & Sons, Inc., 2007), 35.

MUTUAL FUNDS VS INDIVIDUAL STOCKS

Is it possible to beat the general stock market through the purchase of individual stocks? Yes, it is. Through the disciplined use of very demanding principles, some individuals, like Warren Buffett, have been able to exceed the overall return of the stock market over a period of time.

However, if you do not possess the time, ability, or discipline to follow Buffett's very rigorous approach, then a mutual fund is more likely right for you.

Mutual funds offer multiple advantages over individual stocks.

Automatic Diversification

One of the biggest and most widely agreed upon keys to reducing risk in your investments is to diversify your holdings. Common sense tells you that if you put all your eggs in one basket, and that basket is dropped, you've lost all your eggs. It's better to spread your investments out over many different stocks. And unless you are willing and able to do that well through the purchase of many different, quality, individual stocks, a mutual fund is a better choice because it does this for you automatically.

Easy Investment Options

Most mutual fund companies offer simple, easy, and cost-efficient ways for you to invest on a regular basis. Generally, the minimum amount required to start investing is low, and ongoing contributions can usually be as small or large as you want.

In addition, you can normally set up your account so that money is automatically invested on a weekly, bi-weekly, or monthly basis without you having to remember to go in and make the contribution manually.

Time Savings
Because the mutual fund is managed for you, you have nothing to do but make contributions. One rule-of-thumb often given is that a mutual fund investor should only check his investments on New Year's Day and the Fourth of July. If you put any more time into your mutual fund than that, you're probably doing something wrong.

PASSIVE VS ACTIVE
All mutual funds are managed, but how they are managed can make a big difference to your bottom line.

An actively managed fund is a mutual fund where the fund managers are actively and regularly making changes to the fund in an attempt to achieve greater returns. While this may sound good at first, please understand that most fund managers, stock brokers, and financial planners get paid every time a stock is bought or sold (and usually regardless of whether you make money from the transaction or not).

This is true of individual stocks, and it is also true of stocks bought and sold within a mutual fund by the fund managers. Because of this, actively managed mutual funds tend to have higher costs associated with them. And guess who pays for those costs? That's right. You do!

A passively managed fund is a mutual fund where the fund managers generally attempt to make as few changes as possible. These kinds of funds are usually based on a benchmark, standard, or index of some sort (e.g. S&P 500, total stock market, etc.). Therefore, generally speaking, these funds only make changes as changes occur within the holdings or allocations of the benchmark that they are based on. The result for you, as an investor, is that passively managed funds tend to be cheaper.

INDEX VS NON-INDEX

I just mentioned that passively managed funds tend to be based on a benchmark, standard, or index of some sort. These indices are typically tied to a broad market standard such as, for example, the S&P 500 or the total stock market.

For example, an index fund based on the S&P 500 will attempt to replicate the exact holdings and allocations of the S&P 500.[7] In theory then, an index fund should achieve nearly the exact same earnings that the index it is based on achieves. If the S&P 500 is up 6%, then an index fund based on the S&P should, in general, also be up 6%.

WIN WITH THE MARKET

Rather than trying to beat the market (which sounds fun and exciting), the best investors in the world suggest that the average investor (which, most likely, describes you and I and the vast majority of people we know) should be content to track with the market because the market will, over time, likely beat the vast, vast majority of people who try to beat it.

---

[7] Let's pretend that IBM makes up 3% of the total shares within the S&P 500. An index fund based on the S&P 500 would then include IBM as 3% of its total holdings . . . generally replicating the allocation within the index.

It's true. David Swensen, the chief investment officer of the Yale University Endowment Fund, did research which showed that "a miniscule 4% of funds produce market-beating, after-tax results."[8]

Let me translate that for you. After accounting for the cost of taxes on earnings, 96% of funds studied by Mr. Swenson did NOT beat the market!

If I told you that I had a great business opportunity for you that only had a 4% chance of giving you more profit than another business opportunity presented to you, would you choose mine or the other?

When put in those terms, the choice is clear . . . but when it comes to choosing an investment vehicle, far too many people choose the 4% odds over the 96% odds. It's just crazy! Rather than trying to beat the market, the best investors suggest simply choosing to win with the market.

Over time, stocks (in aggregate) have outperformed every other investment option. Alexander Green records a study done by Dr. Jeremy Siegel, a professor of finance at The Wharton School of the University of Pennsylvania, regarding the total returns for various assets over a two-hundred-year period.

> What he discovered is dramatic: $1 invested in gold in 1802 was worth $32.84 at the end of 2006. The same dollar invested in T-bills would have grown to $5,061. $1 invested in bonds would be worth $18,235. And $1 invested in

---

[8] Quoted in Bogle, 33.

common stocks with dividends reinvested – drum roll, please – is worth $12.7 million.[9]

Talk about winning with the market!

You don't have to be a rocket scientist or a financial genius to get these same kinds of results. You just have to be willing to be humble enough and patient enough to let the market do its work.

While it may be boring (and sometimes scary) to just track with the market, remember that you will likely beat the vast, vast majority of those who choose other funds/investments or who try to time/beat the market by using any of the methods Peter Lynch mentioned above.

I don't know about you, but those odds are good enough for me.

_____

[9] Green, 50.

CHAPTER 4
MINIMIZING EXPENSES

There is a lot about investing that you simply cannot control. You can't control returns. You can't control the market. You, sometimes, can't even control how much you can invest.

But one thing you can control is expenses!

In case you're not aware, every investment vehicle (i.e. individual stocks, mutual funds, ETFs, IRAs, etc.) has certain costs directly associated with it.[10] Since I am not an advocate of the buying and selling of individual stocks, I will not address expenses related to that process. For mutual funds, these expenses will normally be labeled as the "expense ratio."

The expense ratio shows how much it is going to cost, on an annual basis, for you to have your mutual fund with the company you choose. More importantly, you must understand that this cost comes directly out of your returns for the year.

For example, let's say you begin the year with $10,000 in a mutual fund that has an expense ratio of 0.5% and that earns a 10% return for the

---

[10] For the sake of this chapter, I am only referring to operating or transaction expenses directly related to the purchase, trading, selling, or holding of various securities. I am not referring to taxes. I will cover how to view and handle taxes in Chapter 5.

year. Your total return would equal $1,000 ($10,000 x 10%) minus $50 ($10,000 x 0.5%) for a total return of $950.[11] Effectively, your 10% rate of return became 9.5% due to the subtraction of the expense ratio.

Imagine if your expense ratio was 1% or 1.5%, and you will begin to see why expense ratios matter so much!

For example, let's assume that that same $10,000 sat untouched for 20 years, and that it had a 10% rate of return every year like clockwork. At an expense ratio of 0.5%, your $10,000 would grow to approximately $61,159 after 20 years. However, under the exact same conditions, if your expense ratio was 1.5%, your $10,000 would only grow to approximately $52,736 – a loss of $8,423 due to nothing but expenses.

Can you begin to see why expenses matter so much? Over the course of your investing life, expenses could eat away $10s or even $100s of thousands of dollars from your overall return.

But here's the kicker: this is totally within your control.

I've already told you that passively managed index funds typically have the lowest expense ratios of any investment vehicle. For example, as of this writing, the average expense ratio for an actively managed large-cap stock fund is 1.25%.[12] Compare that to the expense ratio for the

---

[11] These numbers are not exact, and are for example only.

[12] https://www.thebalance.com/average-expense-ratios-for-mutual-funds-2466612.

passively managed Vanguard® 500 Index Fund (VFIAX) which currently stands at 0.04% - a savings of 1.21%![13]

If you were buying tickets to a movie or concert, and one seller added a 1.25% fee to the cost of your tickets, but another only added a 0.04% fee to the cost of your tickets, which would you choose?

In every other context of life, people tend to pay close attention to (and often make decisions based on) fees and expenses associated with the purchase of various goods or services. But when it comes to investing, many investors act as if they are completely clueless about the effect of fees and expenses on the overall performance of their investments.

Don't be like the average investor. Don't allow fees and expenses to eat away at your returns. While you can't avoid paying for expenses related to owning a mutual fund, you can choose a mutual fund that has the lowest possible expenses.

Failing to do this will be very costly to you in the end.

---

[13] Vanguard® is not a sponsor of this book.

CHAPTER 5
MINIMIZING TAXES

There are three "cost enemies" that every investor faces. The first is inflation. As living expenses go up year after year, our dollars cannot buy as much as they used to. However, there is nothing you or I can do about inflation. We just need to be aware of and plan for it.

The second "cost enemy" that the investor faces is expenses. As discussed in Chapter 4, this is one area of investing where you can exercise a certain amount of control by purposefully choosing investments that have the lowest possible expenses associated with them.

The third "cost enemy" that the investor faces is taxes. Benjamin Franklin said that taxes are one of only two things in life that are certain . . . and he was certainly right.

A good friend of mine once told me that it is a sin to evade taxes . . . but not to avoid them. No one wants to pay taxes, and nobody wants to pay more taxes than they absolutely have to. To the extent that we can find ways to legally and ethically shield our investment returns from taxes, we keep more money in our own pockets.

TAX-DEFERRED ACCOUNTS
The absolute easiest way to minimize the effect of taxes on your investments is by using a tax-deferred account (e.g. IRA, 401(k), SEP, etc.). Earnings or income from investments within tax-deferred accounts will generally not have to be claimed on your yearly tax return.

In theory, you will only be taxed on these earnings when you begin withdrawing money from these accounts in retirement.

Tax Benefits Today
Another benefit of most tax-deferred accounts is that contributions made to them will likely, generally speaking, not be counted as income to you in the year they are made.

For example, let's say Pastor Bob has $25,000 in gross taxable income to report on his 1040. If he contributes $3,000 of that to his traditional IRA, his gross income will likely be adjusted to $22,000.[14]

As another example, let's say Pastor Bob's church makes contributions to a SEP IRA on his behalf of $5,000 a year. That $5,000 should likely not be reported as income on his W2, and will likely therefore not impact his gross taxable income.

This is a major tax benefit!

One exception to this is a Roth IRA. The difference between a traditional and Roth IRA is simple enough to understand. In a traditional IRA, contributions are usually tax-deductible now, grow tax-free over time, but will likely be taxable when withdrawn in retirement.

In a Roth IRA, contributions are not tax-deductible now, but they will grow tax-free over time, and will likely also be tax-free when they are withdrawn in retirement.

---

[14] Assuming he meets contribution limit and rule requirements.

As you can see, either way, you will have to pay taxes – either now or later. You should consult with an accountant or tax professional to determine what is best in your own situation.

Early Withdrawals
Money contributed into a tax-deferred investment account is supposed to remain untouched until you are 59½. At that point, you should be allowed to begin taking penalty-free (but maybe not tax-free) withdrawals.

But what happens if you need or want to take money out of those accounts before you are 59½? Generally speaking, you can expect to pay a 10% penalty tax on the early withdrawal – in addition to extra income taxes that may likely be assessed to you.

That said, there are some situations where you may not be assessed the penalty tax for withdrawing funds early, but you should check with your accountant or tax professional before considering any early withdrawal.[15]

Taxes in Retirement
As stated above, in most tax-deferred accounts, you will pay taxes when you begin withdrawing money from your accounts in retirement at the appropriate tax bracket given all of your income at that time.

---

[15] http://www.schwab.com/public/schwab/investing/retirement_and_planning/understanding_iras/traditional_ira/withdrawal_rules.

The one exception is withdrawals from a Roth account. These withdrawals may be tax-free as long as they are considered to be qualified distributions.[16]

Most Common Types of Tax-Deferred Accounts
The three most common types of tax-deferred accounts are traditional IRAs, Roth IRAs, and employer-sponsored retirement accounts.

I've already mentioned traditional and Roth IRAs multiple times above. These are individual accounts opened directly by the taxpayer. These are very easy to set up, and you have multiple options available to you if you want to establish one today.

The other most common type of tax-deferred account is an employer-sponsored retirement plan. For pastors, this will likely be a SIMPLE IRA, SEP IRA, or 403(b) account.[17] In Chapter 6 of both *How to Not Be a Broke Pastor* and *Structuring Pastoral Compensation*, I explain some of the major differences between these three types of accounts and why, of the three, I prefer SEP accounts for our church and our employees.

For the purposes of this book, all you need to understand is that contributions made into these types of employer-sponsored plans (either by the employer or the employee), as well as earnings from any income within the plan, will likely not be counted as taxable income for the employee. However, as with a traditional IRA, withdrawals made during retirement will likely be taxable.

---

[16] https://www.irs.gov/retirement-plans/traditional-and-roth-iras.
[17] A 403(b) is the non-profit equivalent of a 401(k).

TAXABLE ACCOUNTS

No one is required to use a tax-deferred investment account in order to invest. You could always open an individual account of your own with any investing service. These kinds of accounts do not have the same types of tax benefits that tax-deferred accounts have. In other words, contributions made to taxable accounts will likely not be tax exempt, income generated within the accounts will likely not be tax exempt, and taking a withdrawal through the sale of stock within the fund will likely generate capital gains taxes as well.

If you choose to go this route, this is where you will see the biggest impact from the type of fund you select. If you choose an actively-managed, non-index, mutual fund, you will likely pay more in taxes (and expenses) than you would if you chose a passively-managed, index fund.

The reason for this is because of all of the buying and selling that typically goes on within an actively-managed fund. Each time stocks are sold at a profit within a mutual fund, capital gains taxes are assessed to the fund holders. The more stock that is sold, and the more often stock is sold, the more capital gains taxes may be assessed.

John Bogle estimates that an actively-managed, non-index, mutual fund may generate up to three times the federal taxes for an account holder than a passively-managed index fund.[18] And remember, that's just talking about federal taxes. State and local taxes may add to that difference.

---

[18] Bogle, 62.

It would seem obvious then that, if you were intent on investing in some kind of taxable account, you should definitely choose an investment type that is as tax-efficient as possible.

Similar to what I said about expenses in Chapter 4, the cost of any taxes assessed are basically reducing your overall return. For example, let's imagine that Pastor Bob has taxable investments which earned an annual return of 6%. If taxes eat up 1.5% of his earnings, his effective return becomes 4.5%.[19]

Across town, Pastor George also has taxable investments which earned an annual return of 6%. In his case, he chose more tax-efficient investments which caused his taxes to only eat up 0.75% of his earnings. That means that his effective return becomes 5.25%.[20]

As you may guess, the long-term difference between earning 5.25% and 4.5% will likely be dramatic!

CONCLUSION
While you cannot avoid taxes completely in any investment, you can choose to do things that will, at least, give you some control over when and how much you pay.

Tax-deferred accounts are probably best for most average investors, and you have numerous options within that category to choose from.

---

[19] Not including the cost of any associated management or transactional expenses. This is an over-simplified example.
[20] Again, not including the cost of any associated management or transactional expenses. This is a second, over-simplified example.

But even if you choose taxable accounts, you still have options. You can purposefully choose tax-efficient investments that will generate the least amount of taxes.

Franklin was right. Taxes are certain. My friend was also right. It is a sin to evade them . . . but not to avoid them. You should do everything in your power to minimize your tax burden so that you can keep more of your own money.

CHAPTER 6
BUY AND HOLD FOREVER

Back in Chapter 1, I referenced this old saying: "Buy low; sell high." I then said that, while I generally don't agree with the selling part, I definitely agree with the buying part. Why would I say that?

"Buy low; sell high" is, in fact, a very sound economic policy. If we are going to buy something – a home, a car, stocks, etc. – we should, to the best of our ability, buy it when the price is low. Conversely, if we are planning to sell something, it would be best to do so while the price is high. I take no issue with the economic principle being communicated here.

But when it comes to stocks (or, more precisely, businesses), the best advice seems to be: "Buy low . . . and plan to hold forever."

Don't take my word for it. During a 2015 meeting of "Bogleheads,"[21] John Bogle reminded the audience of his five simple rules for investing: 1) Own the U.S. stock market; 2) Diversify to the "nth" degree; 3) Minimize transaction costs; 4) Have a tiny management expense ratio; and 5) Hold it forever.[22]

---

[21] A self-adopted title for disciples of John Bogle's investment strategy.

[22] http://blog.aarp.org/2015/10/20/jack-bogles-5-simple-rules-for-investing-in-stocks/.

We've already addressed the first four of these. If you own an inexpensive, passively-managed, index fund that is based on something like the S&P 500 or the total U.S. stock market (particularly one held in a tax-deferred account), you will have satisfied the first four pieces of Bogle's advice. But did you notice his fifth piece of advice?

Bogle says that, once you own this type of investment, you should hold it forever! That's right – forever.

But what if the market goes up? Shouldn't you sell high? Or what if it goes down? Shouldn't you get out of stocks before they go any lower?

When asked in a 2016 interview with CNBC about how average investors should view these kinds of situations, Warren Buffett said, "I would tell them, 'Don't watch the market closely.'"[23] He went on to say, "The money is made in investments by investing and by owning good companies for long periods of time. If they buy good companies, buy them over time, they're going to do fine 10, 20, 30 years from now."

He continued: "If they're trying to buy and sell stocks, and worry when they go down a little bit … and think they should maybe sell them when they go up, they're not going to have very good results."

In other words, Buffett, like Bogle, believes that investors should not attempt to buy, sell, or trade stocks based on what the market is doing. Rather, they should make good decisions in regard to what they buy and then hold those investments forever.

---

[23] https://www.cnbc.com/2016/03/04/warren-buffett-buy-hold-and-dont-watch-too-closely.html.

I can hear two questions/objections that may arise at this point.

But What About the Market?

Ahhh . . . the "market" – that unembodied entity that seems to demand so much attention and respect from so many. Shouldn't it be watched? Shouldn't decisions be made based on what is happening in or to the "market"? Let's allow Benjamin Graham to help us answer these questions.

> Imagine that in some private business, you own a small share that cost you $1,000. One of your partners, named Mr. Market, is very obliging indeed. Every day, he tells you what he thinks your interest is worth and furthermore offers to buy you out or to sell you an additional interest on that basis. Sometimes, his idea of value appears plausible and justified by business developments and prospects as you know them. Often, on the other hand, Mr. Market lets his enthusiasm and his fears run away with him, and the value he proposes seems to you a little short of silly.[24]

In other words, and to quote Jason Zweig, Mr. Market can often be manic-depressive and/or bipolar.[25] Occasionally, Mr. Market presents us with a "plausible and justified" value for the various businesses/stocks in it. But more often, Mr. Market acts like a lunatic.

A wise investor shouldn't ignore Mr. Market, but neither should he be controlled by him. When Mr. Market is startled, all the pundits on television chant: "sell, sell, sell." When Mr. Market gets excited, all the

---

[24] Graham, 205.
[25] Graham, 213.

pundits shout: "buy, buy, buy." These are emotional responses, not logical ones.

Do you remember what Buffett said? He said that you need a "sound intellectual framework" and "the ability to keep emotions from corroding that framework."

Giving in to the whims of Mr. Market is the very epitome of the type of corrosion he was referring to. If you have a sound intellectual framework that is guiding your investment decisions, you can begin using what Jason Zweig calls "the most powerful response" any investor could ever give to questions regarding what is happening in the market: "I don't know and I don't care."[26]

Whether or not you know what is happening in the market isn't really the point. The point is that you will not be bullied into making any decisions about your investments based on the, often, wild mood swings of Mr. Market.

DOES "FOREVER" REALLY MEAN FOREVER?
Of course not. No one, not even Warren Buffett, holds on to investments forever. By "forever," he means a really, really long time . . . and not until you have a logical, non-emotional, and compelling reason to sell.

In other words, you should not buy an investment unless you plan to keep it for a really long time, and you should not sell an investment unless and until it fits within the larger "sound intellectual framework" that guides all of your investment decisions.

---

[26] Graham, 131.

THIS IS BORING!

Yes. Yes, it is. Buying inexpensive, passively-managed, index funds that are based on something like the S&P 500 or the total U.S. stock market (particularly ones held in tax-deferred accounts) . . . AND THEN HOLDING THEM FOREVER will give you almost nothing to talk about at dinner parties.

When everyone else is discussing Mr. Market's latest mood swing, you'll likely be quiet. When everyone else is swapping advice about the hottest stocks or the next big thing, you'll have nothing to add.

While "buy and hold forever" may not be very exciting, it is the advice of some of the best, most successful investors of our day, and we would all do well to heed it.

CHAPTER 7
ON ADVISORS AND PROFESSIONALS

Should you work with a certified financial planner or some other kind of advisor to help you with your investments? There is no possible way that I could answer that question for you because there are far too many variables at stake.

WHAT TYPE OF "INVESTOR" ARE YOU?
One of the most helpful sections in *The Intelligent Investor* is Benjamin Graham's distinction between various types of "investors."[27] To begin, I put the word "investor" in quotes because, according to Graham, not everyone who is called an "investor" today is really an investor. Graham writes: "An investment operation is one which, upon thorough analysis, promotes safety of principal and an adequate return. Operations not meeting these requirements are speculative."[28]

Based on that assertion, Graham says that the majority of "investors" today are actually speculators, and not true investors. If I could paraphrase and simplify the distinction between the two, an investor has a "sound intellectual framework" that guides all of his investment decisions, and a speculator does not.

The reason Graham would say that the majority of "investors" today are actually speculators is because they make their investment decisions

---

[27] Graham, 18-34.
[28] Graham, 18.

on ill-informed (or absent) assumptions/information and are also, often, swayed by their own (or Mr. Market's) emotions in decision making. My hope for you is that you would not be (or continue to be) a speculator, but that you would be (or become) a true investor.

In regard to true investors, he further divides this group into two camps: enterprising investors and defensive investors. If I could paraphrase and simplify Graham once more, the difference between these two groups is time and discipline.

An enterprising investor is someone who is both willing and disciplined enough to spend the time needed to do the appropriate research and due diligence required in order to make very detailed and specific decisions related to individual investments. If you are not that . . . you are, by default, a defensive investor.

What does that mean in practical terms? Warren Buffett, Graham's most famous disciple, is an enterprising investor. He has given his life to the disciplined research needed to make very detailed and specific decisions related to individual stocks.

I am a defensive investor. As a pastor, I do not have the time, nor the desire, to do what Buffett does. So, I am content to take the "easier" approach – that of the defensive investor.

A defensive investor is, to put it bluntly, what I have been describing throughout this book. It is a person who is willing to win with the market by investing in inexpensive, passively-managed, index funds that they are willing to hold forever. It really is that simple.

Now that you understand Graham's three types of "investors" – speculators, enterprising investors, and defensive investors – I can make a few comments on the role of advisors for each group.

If you are a speculator, you should definitely use the services of a professional investment advisor. They likely will not know any more than you do about what is going to happen next with any particular stock or with the market as a whole, but maybe they can give you some pointers from their own experience.

If you are an enterprising investor, you should probably use the services of a professional investment advisor. I think the reasons for why you would use an advisor are very different than that of a speculator, but I could see how their services would greatly benefit an investor of this type – particularly for the research aspect of your decisions.

However, if you are a defensive investor, I think you can use the services of a professional investment advisor, but I don't believe that you absolutely have to. The answer to that question is somewhat dependent on your temperament.

WHAT IS YOUR TEMPERAMENT?
Do you remember this comment by Graham: "We have seen much more money made and *kept* by 'ordinary people' who were temperamentally well suited for the investment process than by those who lacked this quality, even though they had an extensive knowledge of finance, accounting, and stock market lore."[29]

---

[29] Graham, 8. Emphasis his.

What quality did those other, more seemingly-qualified people lack? In Graham's mind, they lacked a certain temperament. The temperament Graham is referring to is the ability to follow your plan (your "sound intellectual framework") without being derailed by your own emotions.

If you are that type of person – if that is your temperament – then you may not need the help of a professional investment advisor. You may be able to do the things suggested by Graham, Buffett, and others on your own.

But if you are not that type of person, and there is a danger that you could be tempted to veer off-track if left to your own devices, then the right professional investment advisor may be able to help "talk you off the ledge" when those moments come.

A FEW THOUGHTS ON FEES

Regardless of which type of investor you are or what your temperament is, if you choose to work with an advisor or professional of some sort, be mindful of the fees being charged. As we talked about in Chapter 4, fees or expenses associated with your investments have the effect of directly reducing your returns. This is true regardless of how the fees/expenses are charged. You may not be able to avoid these expenses if you choose to hire a professional, but you can choose someone with the lowest possible fees.

As I said, in the end, I cannot tell you whether or not you should work with a certified financial planner or some other kind of advisor to help you with your investments. But I hope that, now, you will have a better framework for making this important decision.

CHAPTER 8
MY APPROACH

Having shared all of the advice above, what do I do? I'm not sharing this with you as a way of saying that you should make the same decisions I have made. I am simply sharing my own approach so that you can see one example of how one pastor is putting these principles to work.

My approach is very simple: I only invest in passively-managed index funds held within tax-deferred accounts that I have no plans on touching until I get to retirement.

As it stands right now, my wife and I have four investment accounts - two each - all with Vanguard®.[30] For me, I have a traditional IRA and a SEP IRA (provided for me by our church). My wife also has a traditional IRA and an i401(k).[31] In each of these four accounts, we have invested in the same index fund: the Vanguard® Target Retirement 2045 Fund (VTIVX). We do not work with an advisor or certified financial planner. With the exception of the SEP IRA, we opened and continue to manage these accounts ourselves.

---

[30] While I have chosen to work with Vanguard®, personally, Vanguard® is not a sponsor of this book, and there are other good companies out there that offer similar products to Vanguard®.

[31] An i401(k) is an individual 401(k) for sole-proprietors (my wife is self-employed).

The reason we choose the Vanguard® Target Retirement 2045 Fund is because it is an index fund that automatically rebalances itself over time as we get closer to retirement and because the expense ratio for this fund is only 0.16%. Currently, the balance is 90% stocks and 10% bonds.

Every month, we make automatic contributions to both of our traditional IRAs regardless of what is happening in the market. In addition, the church makes regular monthly contributions to my SEP, and my wife makes regular monthly contributions to her i401(k).

Because all four of these accounts are tax-deferred, we reap tremendous tax savings from them. Not only are our contributions tax-deferred or tax-deductible now, but all of the earnings and growth within the funds are non-taxable.

Do I care what happens in the markets? Yes and no. Since I make the same contribution amounts every month, I am thankful for the months when the market is down because that allows me to buy more stock than I can buy in months when the market is up. In this sense, I care about market price. But in the sense of what is happening in the overall market, I don't care. Whether the market is up or down, I still own the same amount of business that I did before, and I'm going to buy more no matter what.

And . . . that's pretty much it. I told you it was boring.

Is this a crazy approach? I don't think so. The particular fund and approach I've chosen is very similar to what Warren Buffett has instructed for his wife's provision after his death:

What I advise here is essentially identical to certain instructions I've laid out in my will. One bequest provides that cash will be delivered to a trustee for my wife's benefit...My advice to the trustee could not be more simple: Put 10% of the cash in short-term government bonds and 90% in a very low-cost S&P 500 index fund. (I suggest Vanguard®'s.) I believe the trust's long-term results from this policy will be superior to those attained by most investors...[32]

If that's good enough for Buffett's wife, then it's good enough for me!

Even though I may not, personally, know much about stocks or investing or retirement, I feel fairly confident that men like Buffett, Bogle, Graham, and others like them do; and I am more than content to both listen to and follow their advice for myself and my family.

---

[32] https://www.forbes.com/sites/davidwismer/2014/03/02/warren-buffett-investing-advice-for-you-and-my-wife-and-other-quotes-of-the-week/#48b5d8fd6e2c.

FINAL THOUGHTS

As I said at the beginning, I don't know anything about investing, and I did not write this book to promote my own views of how you should prepare for retirement.

However, I do believe that every pastor should be preparing for retirement; and if you, like me, know nothing about investing, then what I have done is given you the best advice I have found from the some of the best investors of our day for your consideration.

Most people like new and exciting things, but as you can see, none of what these giants of investing have said is either new or exciting. In fact, it's quite boring. It's dull. It's mundane. It's so "common-sense" that it almost seems too simple.

And yet, I am trusting that these individuals know more than I do. Therefore, I have made my decisions based off of their advice.

I pray that God will grant you wisdom and clarity as you seek to make your own decisions about your retirement and your future.

brokepastor

Visit www.brokepastor.com, the #1 online resource for understanding pastoral compensation and finance issues, for more topics, information, and resources that you can actually use.

Don't be a **BROKE PASTOR**

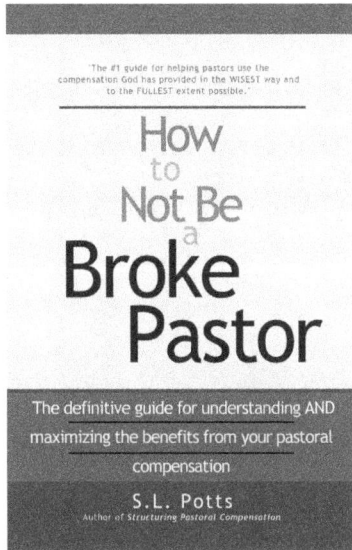

Are you struggling to understand the unique and challenging world of pastoral compensation? Are you maximizing the benefits that could be yours by simply being "wise as a serpent and innocent as a dove" when it comes to how you structure your pastoral pay?

As a pastor, I get it. Not only can our compensation be confusing, but there are also so many different components that need to be balanced . . . it can be hard to put all the pieces together.

How to Not Be a Broke Pastor is written for pastors/ministers and is designed to make the complexities of clergy pay simple and easy to understand, and also to give you ideas as to how you can use your income to the greatest extent possible.

Bless Your Pastor!

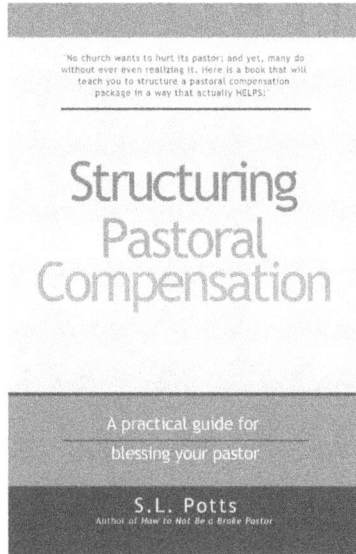

'No church wants to hurt its pastor; and yet, many do without ever even realizing it. Here is a book that will teach you to structure a pastoral compensation package in a way that actually HELPS.'

Structuring
Pastoral
Compensation

A practical guide for
blessing your pastor

S.L. Potts
Author of How to Not Be a Broke Pastor

Is your church structuring its pastoral compensation package in a way that truly blesses your pastor? Is your church doing all it can and should to financially provide for the pastors who keep watch over your souls?

The fact of the matter is that most churches have never given any thought to what a pastoral compensation package should look like, and much less to how they should structure it so that their pastor receives the maximum benefit.

Structuring Pastoral Compensation is written for church decision makers (Elders, Deacons, Trustees, Committee Members, etc.) to help them understand what should be included in their pastor's compensation and how to best implement the various pieces so that their pastor will be truly blessed.

Could your church save
$100,000 or more?

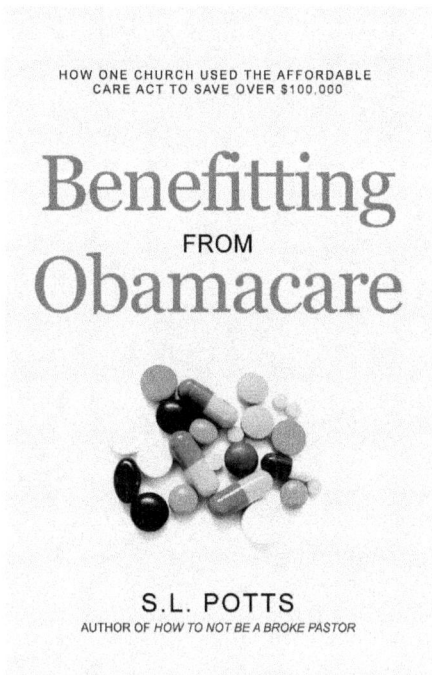

HOW ONE CHURCH USED THE AFFORDABLE
CARE ACT TO SAVE OVER $100,000

Benefitting
FROM
Obamacare

S.L. POTTS
AUTHOR OF *HOW TO NOT BE A BROKE PASTOR*

Over the past three years, our church has saved over $100,000 in health insurance premiums by using the provisions of the Affordable Care Act (a.k.a Obamacare) to our advantage - $100,000 that we have used to hire additional staff, send one of our members into foreign missions, and pay down our church's mortgage!

Written for both pastors and church decision makers, *Benefitting from Obamacare* is the story of how we did that, the challenges we faced, the things we had to consider, and what we have experienced since.